KRISHNA AND THE FALSE VAASUDEVA

A MESSENGER FROM JARASANDHA, THE EMPEROR OF MAGADHA, CAME TO THE COURT OF VAASUDEVA, THE MIGHTY, BUT STUPID KING OF PUNDRA*.

THE EMPEROR'S FAVOURITE VASSAL, LORD SHISHUPALA⁵, IS GOING TO WED RUKMINI, THE PRINCESS OF VIDARBHA...

THAT PEERLESS BEAUTY! GOOD NEWS, INDEED!

THE EMPEROR WANTS ALL HIS ALLIES TO COME PREPARED FOR BATTLE. HE EXPECTS TROUBLE FROM THAT YADAVA, KRISHNA.◉

BUT HASN'T RUKMI*PROMISED HIS SISTER TO SHISHUPALA?

HE HAS! AND THERE IS NOT GOING TO BE A SWAYAMVARA BUT...

...ONE CAN NEVER BE SURE! THE YADAVA MAY DECIDE THAT HE WANTS RUKMINI FOR HIMSELF.

NOT AS LONG AS I LIVE!

WHEN VAASUDEVA AND HIS ARMY REACHED VIDARBHA, JARASANDHA AND HIS ALLIES WERE ALREADY THERE. AMONG THEM WAS VAASUDEVA'S CLOSE FRIEND, THE KING OF KASHI.

EVERYTHING SEEMS TO BE ALL RIGHT. THERE IS NO SIGN OF THE YADAVA.

*RUKMINI'S BROTHER

EVEN IF HE DOES COME, WE WILL NOT LET HIM GET ANYWHERE NEAR THE PRINCESS. WE WILL NOT FAIL SHISHUPALA AND THE EMPEROR!

THE NEXT MORNING, SHISHUPALA AND THE ASSEMBLED KINGS WAITED PATIENTLY FOR RUKMINI TO EMERGE FROM THE TEMPLE WHERE SHE HAD GONE TO WORSHIP BEFORE THE WEDDING CEREMONY.

AS RUKMINI CAME OUT, SO DAZZLED WERE THEY BY HER BEAUTY THAT THEY STOOD STARING AT HER, HARDLY AWARE OF ANYTHING ELSE!

SUDDENLY, AS IF FROM NOWHERE, KRISHNA APPEARED IN HIS CHARIOT...

...WHISKED RUKMINI INTO IT...

...AND DROVE OFF!

STOP HIM!

HE HAS ABDUCTED THE PRINCESS!

LITTLE DID THEY REALISE THAT RUKMINI HAD MADE HER OWN CHOICE AND HER OWN PLANS.

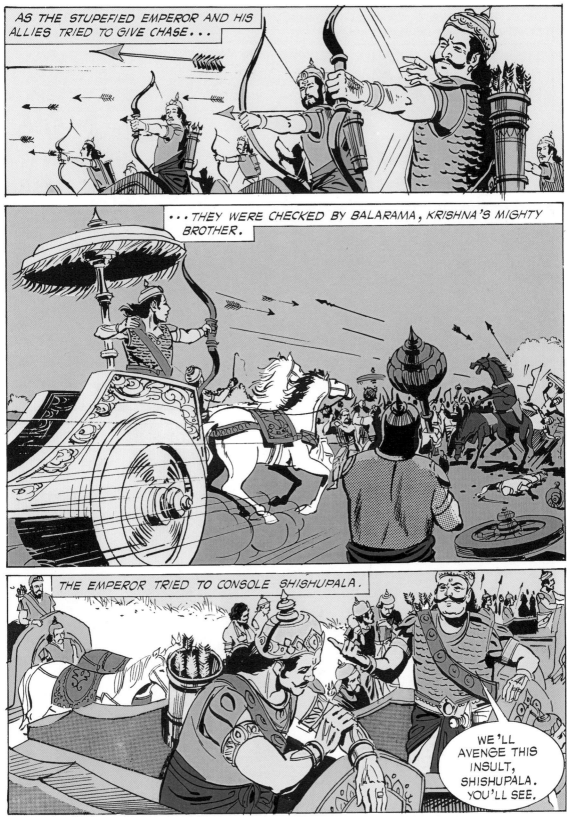

AS THE STUPEFIED EMPEROR AND HIS ALLIES TRIED TO GIVE CHASE...

...THEY WERE CHECKED BY BALARAMA, KRISHNA'S MIGHTY BROTHER.

THE EMPEROR TRIED TO CONSOLE SHISHUPALA.

WE'LL AVENGE THIS INSULT, SHISHUPALA. YOU'LL SEE.

5

WHILE THE EMPEROR PLANNED REVENGE, VAASUDEVA RETURNED TO HIS CAPITAL, A DEJECTED MAN.

HE WAS ONE AND WE WERE MANY. YET HE CARRIED OFF RUKMINI! UNDER OUR VERY NOSE!

HIS COURTIERS WERE WORRIED.

THIS WILL NEVER DO! IF THE KING REMAINS SO LISTLESS, THE KINGDOM WILL BE OPEN TO INVADERS AND OUR PEOPLE WILL BECOME SLAVES.

IT'S THAT KRISHNA WHO HAS DONE THIS TO HIM.

7

WE ONLY HAVE TO CONVINCE THE PEOPLE AND SOON OUR KING WILL COME TO BELIEVE IT HIMSELF.

AND IN NO TIME HE WILL REGAIN HIS SELF-CONFIDENCE.

THE COURTIERS SET TO WORK.

...HE IS THE TRUE VAASUDEVA! KRISHNA IS AN IMPOSTOR!

IT CAN'T BE TRUE!

OUR KING IS VAASUDEVA, LORD VISHNU INCARNATE!

KRISHNA IS AN IMPOSTOR!

AS TIME ROLLED BY—

AM I REALLY LORD VISHNU INCARNATE? THE PEOPLE COULD NOT BE MISTAKEN. I MUST BE VISHNU REBORN.

AND THE KING BELIEVED HIMSELF TO BE VISHNU. AND HE BEGAN TO DRESS LIKE KRISHNA, THE VAASUDEVA.

HOW DARE THAT YADAVA CALL HIMSELF VAASUDEVA! THE IMPOSTOR!

AND THAT IMPOSTOR HAS MY DISCUS AND INSIGNIA.

ONE DAY—

GO TO DWARAKA AND GIVE KRISHNA THIS MESSAGE...

A FEW DAYS LATER AT DWARAKA—

LORD, AN AMBASSADOR FROM THE COURT OF VAASUDEVA, KING OF PUNDRA, SEEKS AN AUDIENCE.

SHOW HIM IN.

MY NAMESAKE IS AN ALLY OF JARASANDHA AND SHISHUPALA. WHAT COULD HE WANT WITH ME?

HIS QUESTION WAS SOON ANSWERED.

OUR DIVINE KING, VISHNU INCARNATE, SAYS: " COME TO PUNDRA AND GIVE UP MY DISCUS, YOU FOOLISH MAN. LAY ASIDE MY INSIGNIA AND MY NAME. IF YOU COME AND PAY HOMAGE TO ME, I WILL VOUCHSAFE YOUR SAFETY."

KRISHNA WAS AMUSED.

OH! SO THAT'S IT! VAASUDEVA HAS DIVINE DESIGNS!

GO TO VAASUDEVA AND TELL HIM THIS FROM ME···

WHEN THE MESSENGER RETURNED TO PUNDRA—

WHAT DID HE SAY? WAS HE ANGRY?

NO, MY LORD. HE SAID SINCE YOU COMMAND HIM TO COME, HE WILL OBEY IMMEDIATELY. HE WILL BRING THE DISCUS, HIS EMBLEM, AND CONSIGN IT TO YOU. AND···

···SEEKING ASYLUM WITH YOU, HE WILL ENSURE THAT HE WILL NEVER MORE HAVE ANYTHING TO DREAD FROM YOU.

WHAT! IS KRISHNA GIVING IN SO EASILY? I AM INDEED FORTUNATE!

13

BUT HIS COURTIERS DID NOT THINK SO.

I DON'T TRUST THAT YADAVA!

YES. THERE IS MORE TO THIS THAN MEETS THE EYE!

WHY NOT SEND A MESSENGER TO THE KING OF KASHI AND SEEK HIS ADVICE? EVEN INDRA, KING OF THE DEVAS, FEARS HIM.

WHEN THE KING OF KASHI HEARD THE WHOLE STORY—

VAASUDEVA OF PUNDRA DOESN'T REALISE WHAT HE HAS DONE! WOULD HE WHO HAS HUMBLED THE EMPEROR HIMSELF SURRENDER TO A MERE KING AND SEEK HIS PROTECTION?

I HAD BETTER GO WITH MY TROOPS AND MYSELF TAKE ON THE REARGUARD. THE KING OF PUNDRA IS GOING TO NEED US.

HE SENT FOR HIS SON, SUDAKSHINA.

KRISHNA THE YADAVA, MUST BE TAUGHT A LESSON AND I AM GOING TO HELP THE KING OF PUNDRA TEACH IT TO HIM. LOOK AFTER THE KINGDOM WHILE I AM AWAY.

MEANWHILE KRISHNA, MOUNTED ON GARUDA, WAS WELL ON HIS WAY TO PUNDRA, WITH HIS MACE, DISCUS AND BOW.

15

SOON THE EARTH WAS STREWN WITH THE BODIES OF THE TWO ARMIES AND THEIR HORSES AND ELEPHANTS.

VAASUDEVA, YOU WANTED ME TO HAND OVER MY INSIGNIA!

BUT THE WARNING WAS TOO LATE. KRISHNA'S MACE HIT VAASUDEVA, HURLING HIM TO THE GROUND.

THE NEXT MOMENT THE DISCUS CUT HIS THROAT, AND VAASUDEVA WAS NO MORE.

THE GARUDA ON HIS BANNER WAS SHATTERED TO BITS BY KRISHNA'S GARUDA.

AS KRISHNA TURNED ROUND, THE KING OF KASHI ACCOSTED HIM.

WELL DONE, KRISHNA! BUT DON'T FORGET, I'M STILL ALIVE.

WHY DON'T YOU FIGHT ME, YOU IMPOSTOR?

KRISHNA ONLY SMILED IN REPLY...

...AND RAISING HIS BOW LET FLY AN ARROW.

THE NEXT MOMENT THE HEAD OF THE KING OF KASHI WAS SEVERED FROM THE BODY.

BUT THE MOMENTUM OF THE ARROW WAS SO GREAT THAT IT CARRIED THE HEAD OF THE KING WITH IT···

···AND DISAPPEARED INTO SPACE.

A VICTORIOUS KRISHNA RETURNED TO DWARAKA WHERE HE WAS RECEIVED BY HIS REJOICING SUBJECTS.

MEANWHILE, THE ARROW CARRYING THE HEAD OF THE KING OF KASHI, WHIZZED THROUGH THE AIR...

...TILL IT REACHED THE PALACE GATES OF THE CITY OF KASHI.

OUR KING HAS BEEN SLAIN. ALAS!

ALAS!

ALAS!

WHEN SUDAKSHINA, THE SON OF THE KING OF KASHI, HEARD THEIR CRIES, HE CAME OUT OF THE PALACE.

IT IS THE WORK OF KRISHNA OF DWARAKA. I WILL NOT REST TILL I SEE HIM DEAD.

ALONG WITH HIS FAMILY PRIEST, SUDAKSHINA BEGAN TO PERFORM A YAGNA.

SWAHA!

SUDDENLY THE SACRIFICIAL FIRE BLAZED HIGH...

... AND FROM IT EMERGED A FORMIDABLE FEMALE, WITH FLAMES OF FIRE LEAPING OUT OF HER HAIR.

23

ROARING ANGRILY, SHE CHARGED THROUGH THE AIR TOWARDS DWARAKA.

MEANWHILE AT DWARAKA, KRISHNA WAS PLAYING DICE WITH RUKMINI.

SUDDENLY —

LORD SAVE US!

A FIERY FIEND IS HEADING TOWARDS DWARAKA.

SHE ROARS THAT SHE WON'T REST TILL DWARAKA WITH ALL ITS INHABITANTS IS RAZED TO THE GROUND.

TURNING, THE FIEND FLED.

BUT THE DISCUS PURSUED HER RELENTLESSLY.

AH! THE CITY OF SUDAKSHINA. SINCE IT WAS SUDAKSHINA WHO BROUGHT ME TO THIS PLIGHT, I WILL SLAY HIM.

MEANWHILE SUDAKSHINA AND HIS ARMIES HAD ALREADY BEGUN RESISTING THE DISCUS...

...BUT IN VAIN. THE DISCUS ATTACKED THEM WITH A VENGEANCE, FELLING THEM IN ALL DIRECTIONS. TILL...

...THE LAST OF SUDAKSHINA'S SOLDIERS FELL.

SUDAKSHINA FLED FROM THE BATTLE-FIELD TO HIS PALACE.

MEANWHILE THE FIEND TOO HAD REACHED THE PALACE.

YOU SHALL DIE FOR BEING THE CAUSE OF MY HUMILIATION!

AND SUDAKSHINA WAS BURNT TO DEATH BY THE CREATURE HIS OWN INCANTATIONS HAD BROUGHT FORTH.

SUDDENLY—

NO! IT'S THE SUDARSHANA-CHAKRA AGAIN! IT HAS PURSUED ME INTO THE CITY.

AS THE DISCUS APPROACHED, THE FIEND FLED...

...AND CONCEALED *HERSELF* IN THE CITY.

THE BLAZING DISCUS WHIRRED THROUGH PALACE ASSEMBLY HALLS...

... TILL THE WHOLE CITY OF KASHI WAS WRAPPED UP IN FLAMES ...

... WHICH CONSUMED EVEN THE FUGITIVE FIEND.

THE DISCUS, THEN, WITH UNMITIGATED VIGOUR AND BLAZING FIERCELY, WHIRLED AROUND AND...

...WHIZZED BACK TO THE PALACE AT DWARAKA...

...TO THE HANDS OF THE TRUE VAASUDEVA.

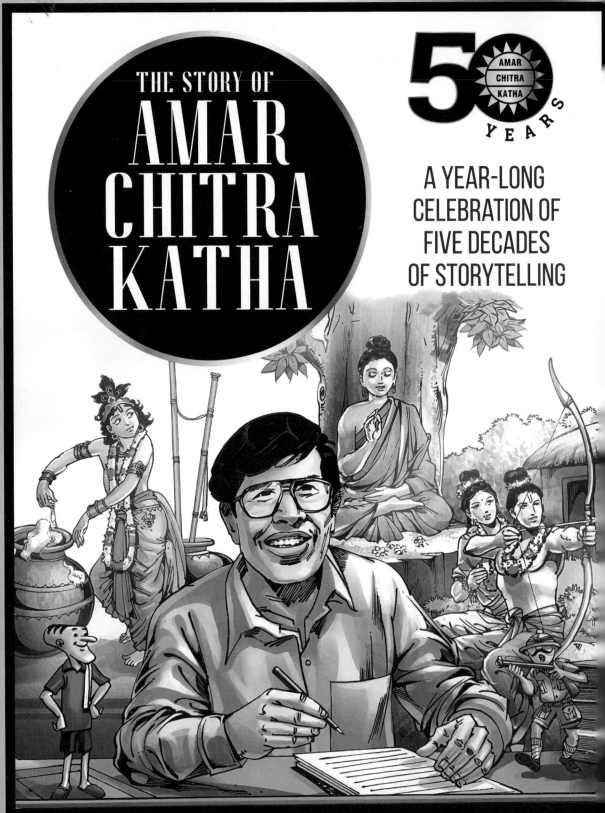

THE STORY OF
AMAR CHITRA KATHA

50 YEARS
AMAR CHITRA KATHA

A YEAR-LONG CELEBRATION OF FIVE DECADES OF STORYTELLING

WE PROUDLY PRESENT A SERIALISED RETELLING OF HOW OUR BELOVED FOUNDER, UNCLE PAI, FIRST STARTED AMAR CHITRA KATHA AND TINKLE!

LOOK OUT FOR A ONE-PAGE COMIC IN EVERY ISSUE THIS YEAR!